Herbert Puchta Günter Gerngross Peter Lewis-Jones

Super Minds

American English

Student's Book 1

CAMBRIDGE
UNIVERSITY PRESS

Map of the book

Friends (pages 4–9)

Vocabulary	Grammar	Story and value	Thinking skills
Greetings Numbers 1–10 Colors	*What's your name?* *I'm (Thunder).* *How old are you?* *I'm (seven).*	*Meet the Super Friends* Making friends	• Matching

▶ **Song:** A, B, C, D, E, F, G

① At school (pages 10–21)

Vocabulary	Grammar	Story and value Phonics	Skills	Thinking skills	English for school
Classroom objects	*What's this? It's a (pencil).* *Is it a pen? Yes, it is. / No, it isn't.* *Open your book, please.*	*Watch out, Flash!* Helping each other The letter sound *a*	• Listening • Reading, speaking, and writing	• Matching • Hypothesizing and predicting	**Art:** Colors

▶ **Song:** What's this?   ▶ **Creativity**   ▶ **Review**

② Let's play! (pages 22–33)

Vocabulary	Grammar	Story and value Phonics	Skills	Thinking skills	English for school
Toys	*What's his/her name?* *His/Her name's (Ben/Sue).* *What's his/her favorite toy?* *How old is he/she?* *It's a (new kite).* *It's an (ugly monster).*	*The go-cart race* Fair play – cheating is wrong The letter sound *e*	• Reading • Listening, speaking, and writing	• Comparative thinking • Analysis of statements • Hypothesizing	**Math:** Tangrams

▶ **Song:** Hey, Emma! What's your favorite toy?   ▶ **Creativity**   ▶ **Review**

③ Pet show (pages 34–45)

Vocabulary	Grammar	Story and value Phonics	Skills	Thinking skills	English for school
Animals	*The (lizard) is in/on/under the (bag).* *I like / don't like (dogs).*	*The spider* Being brave The letter sound *i*	• Reading, listening, and writing • Speaking	• Matching • Applying world knowledge	**Science:** Camouflage

▶ **Song:** Look at the spiders   ▶ **Creativity**   ▶ **Review**

④ Lunchtime (pages 46–57)

Vocabulary	Grammar	Story and value Phonics	Skills	Thinking skills	English for school
Food	*I have / don't have a (sandwich).* *Do we have any (cheese)?* *Yes, we do. / No, we don't.*	*The pizza* Waiting your turn The letter sound *o*	• Listening and writing • Reading and speaking	• Categorizing • Applying world knowledge • Predicting	**Science:** Fruit and veg

▶ **Song:** Tommy's in the kitchen   ▶ **Creativity**   ▶ **Review**

Friends

1 🎧 CD1 02 **Listen and look. Then listen and say the words.**

1 Whisper   **2** Thunder   **3** Misty   **4** Flash

2 🎧 CD1 03 **Listen and chant.**

Hi, I'm Whisper.
What's your name?
Hi, I'm Thunder.
What a nice name!

Hi, I'm Flash.
What's your name?
Hi, I'm Misty.
What a nice name!

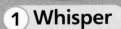

1 **CD1 04** **Listen and point to the numbers.**

2 **CD1 05** **How old are the Super Friends? Listen and write.**

I'm _____ .

I'm _____ .

I'm _____ .

I'm _____ .

3 **Ask and answer.**

What's your name?

How old are you?

I'm Carlos.

I'm six.

1 CD1 06 **Listen and sing.**

A, B, C, D, E, F, G
Sing with me ...

H, I, J, K, L, M, N
I'm your friend ...

O, P, Q, and R, and S
Yes, yes, yes ...
T, U, V, and W
Me and you ...

X, Y, and Z
Let's sing and dance.
X, Y, and Z
The alphabet ...

2 **Say the alphabet.**

A

B

1 CD1 08 **Listen and point to the balloons.**

yellow
red
orange
purple
blue
green

2 CD1 09 **Listen and color. Then follow the lines and say.**

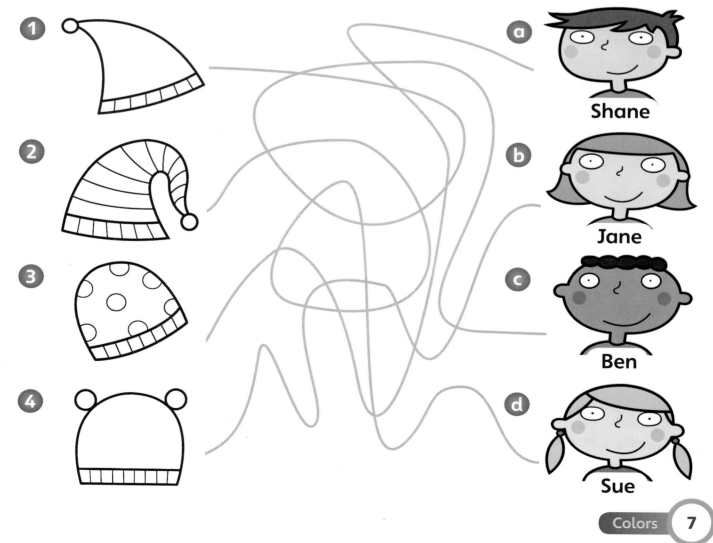

1

2

3

4

a Shane

b Jane

c Ben

d Sue

2 **Think!** **Read and number the pictures.**

1 Look at me! **2** My turn. Look! **3** I'm Tabby.

4 How old are you? **5** No. Listen to me!

1 At school

1 CD1 12 **Listen and look. Then listen and say the words.**

1 pen
2 eraser
3 pencil
4 book
5 notebook
6 bag
7 desk
8 ruler
9 pencil case

2 CD1 13 **Listen and chant.**

Hey, Flash! Hey, Flash!
Come back, come back!

Your ruler, your eraser,
Your pencil, your book,
Your pen,
And your pencil case.

Hey, Flash! Hey, Flash!
Close your bag, close your bag!

Your ruler, your eraser,
Your pencil, your book,
Your pen,
And your pencil case.

1 CD1 14 Listen and number the pictures.

What's this?

It's a ruler.

What's this?

Is it a pencil?

No, it isn't. It's a pen.

What's this?

Yes, it is.

Is it a pencil case?

What's this?

Is it an eraser?

Yes, it is.

2 CD1 15 Grammar focus   Listen and say.

What's this?	**It's a pencil.**
No, **it isn't.**	**Is it a pen?**
Yes, **it is.**	

3 Play the guessing game.

What's this?

Is it a … ?

1 CD1 17 **Listen and sing.**

What's this?

Look at the desk,
Look at the desk,
The desk is a mess!

Is it your pen?
Is it your book?
Is it your pencil case?

Yes or no?
Tell me, Joe.

It isn't my pen.
It isn't my book.
It isn't my pencil case.
Oh, no, no!
No, no, no!

Look at the desk ...

2 **Look at Joe's desk. Draw lines from the school things to the correct desk.**

1 CD 1 19 **Listen and stick.**
Then write the words.

pen   book   bag   desk

1 Sit at your _____, please.

2 Open your _____, please.

3 Close your _____, please.

4 Pass me a _____, please.

Here you go.

2 CD 1 20 **Grammar focus**   **Listen and say.**

Open your book, please.   **Pass** me a ruler, please.
Sit at your desk, please.   **Close** your bag, please.

3 **Play the chain game.**

Open your …

Pass me …

Watch out, Flash!

2 **Think!** **Find and circle the same pictures in the story.**

3 **Find who says ...** My bag!

4 CD 1 23 **Listen and say.**

A fat rat in a black bag.

 Listen and draw lines.

Sam

Fred

Kim

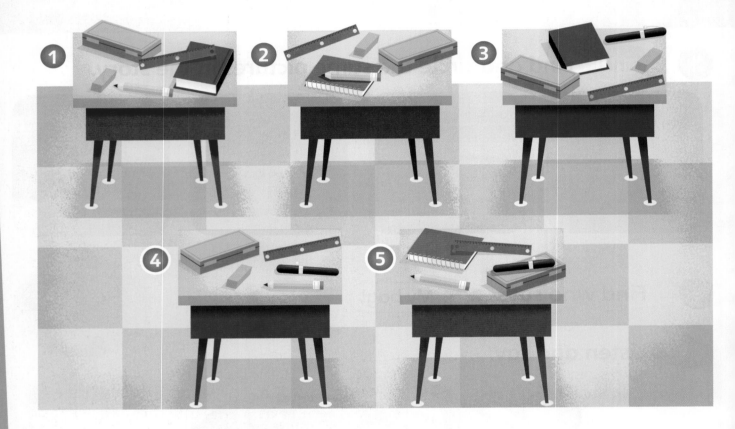

Mia

Jane

Skills

1 **Read and circle the correct pictures.**

1  Put away your book, please.

2  Take out your ruler, please.

3  Pass me a pencil, please.

4 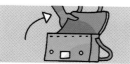 Open your bag, please.

2 **Ask and answer.** What's number one?  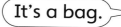 It's a bag.

1 **2** **3**

4 **5** **6**

3 **Draw and write about your bag.**

This is my bag.
It is green and blue.

1 Read and answer the questions.

a There are three primary colors. What are they?

b Look at your classroom. What objects are blue, red, or yellow?

2 Look and read. Mix the colors to make new colors.

We mix the primary colors to make new colors. These are called secondary colors.

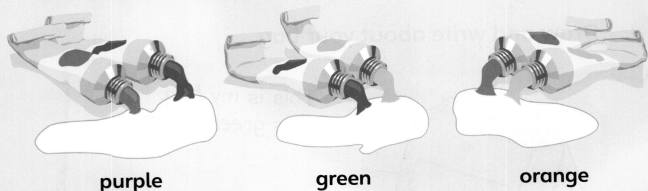

purple   green   orange

1 Look at the picture. Read and answer.

a Find the primary colors. What are they?

b Find the secondary colors. Do you remember how to make them?

2 Think! When you mix white with a different color, the color gets lighter. Look, think, and color.

1 White + Red = ?   **2** White + Black = ?

3 Project Make your own picture.

1 CD1 27 **Listen and act it out with your teacher. Then listen again and number the pictures.**

2 **Read and number the sentences from the story.**

Look down and catch it.

Take out your pencil case.

Put the pencil case on your head.

Turn around.

Stand up.

Stretch.

3 **Listen to your friend and act it out.**

Put the ruler on your head.

1 Make a poster.

Colors at school

a Write the color words on your poster.

b Think of school objects and find pictures in different colors.

c Cut out the pictures and stick them on your poster.

PRIMARY   SECONDARY

2 Count the school objects. Close your eyes. What color are they?

> There are nine pencils. Two are blue and two are red ...

2 Let's play!

1 🔊 CD1 28 **Listen and look. Then listen and say the words.**

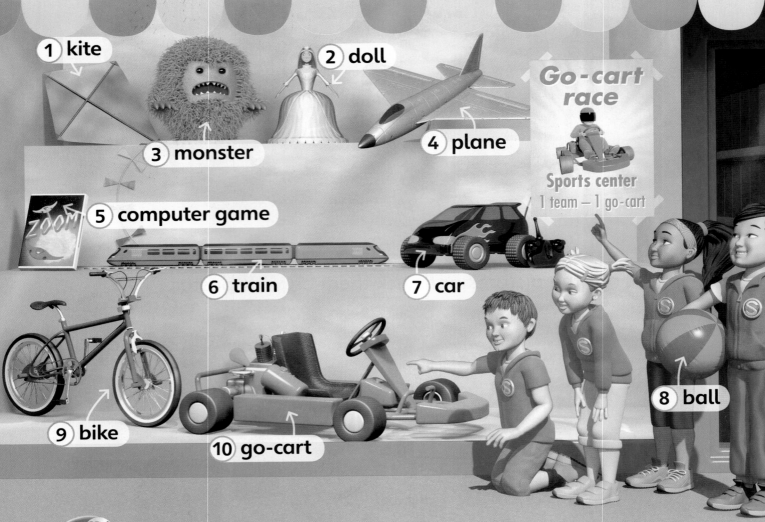

1 kite
2 doll
3 monster
4 plane
5 computer game
6 train
7 car
8 ball
9 bike
10 go-cart

Go-cart race
Sports center
1 team — 1 go-cart

2 🔊 CD1 29 **Listen and chant.**

Toy store, toy store,
Let's go to the toy store.
Look!

A doll, a car, a bike, oh, yes,
A go-cart, and a train,

A ball, a computer game,
A monster, and a plane.

Yes.
And there's a kite!
That's right!

1 ^{CD 1} 31 **Listen and stick.**

Sticker

1

Sophie

2

Alex

3

Olivia

4

Mark

2 ^{CD 1} 32 **Grammar focus** **Listen and say.**

What's **his** name?	**His** name's Ben.
How old is **he**?	**He**'s seven.
What's **his** favorite toy?	**His** favorite toy's **his** ball.
What's **her** name?	**Her** name's Lisa.
How old is **she**?	**She**'s six.
What's **her** favorite toy?	**Her** favorite toy's **her** doll.

3 **Ask and answer.**

What's … ?

How … ?

What's his/her … ? How old is he/she? **23**

1  **Listen and sing.**

Hey, Emma! What's your favorite toy? ...

My favorite toy isn't a plane.
It isn't a kite or a computer game.
My favorite toy!

Hey, Mike! What's your favorite number? ...

My favorite number isn't three.
Can you find it? Look at me!
My favorite number!

Hey, Emma! What's your favorite toy? ...

My favorite toy ...
My favorite toy's a go-cart.
That's smart!

Hey, Mike! What's your favorite number? ...

My favorite number ...
My favorite number's eight.
That's great!

2 **Look at the picture. Find and circle Emma and Mike.**

1 CD 1 35 **Listen and number the pictures.**

A long
blue train.

A short
red train.

A big
green ball.

A small
yellow ball.

An ugly purple
monster.

A beautiful
orange monster.

An old black
go-cart.

A new pink
go-cart.

2 CD 1 36 **Grammar focus** **Listen and say.**

It's **a new** kite.   It's **an ugly** monster.

3 **Draw a toy. Ask and answer.**

Is it a monster?

Yes, it is.

No, it isn't.

Is it green?

2 Think! Read and number the go-carts.

1 A small go-cart.   **2** An old go-cart.   **3** A new go-cart.

3 Find who says ...   This is Ben from the Red team.

4 Listen and say.   CD1 40

Ken and his ten red pencils.

1 **Look and read. Check (✓) or put an X.**

1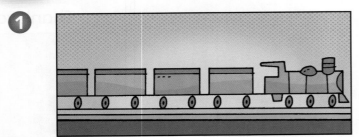

It's a long train. ☐

2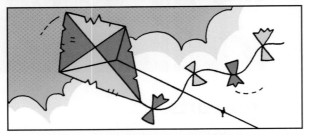

It's a new kite. ☐

3

It's a big boat. ☐

4

It's an ugly doll. ☐

5

It's an old bike. ☐

6

It's a short train. ☐

Skills

1 CD 1 43 **Listen and write the names.**

Beep   Dino   Nessie   Star

1

2

3

4

2 **Ask and answer.**

What's your favorite   toy?
color?
number?

My favorite ...

3 **Draw and write about your favorite toy.**

My favorite things.
My favorite toy is my blue doll.

Tangrams

1 CD 1 44 **Listen and look at the shapes.**

Can you see them in your classroom?

My book is a rectangle.

1

triangle

2

square

3

circle

4

parallelogram

5

rectangle

2 **Read and answer.**

The tangram is an old Chinese toy.
Look at the tangram. What shapes can
you see? What shapes can't you see?

I can see a square. I can't see a circle.

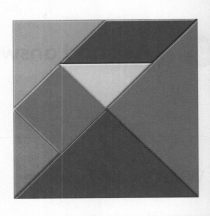

3 **Think!** **Look at the tangrams. What shapes are missing?**

The blue triangle is missing.

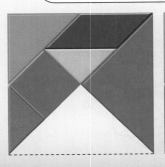 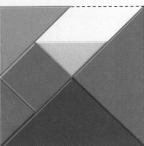 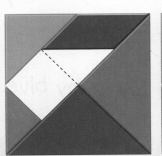 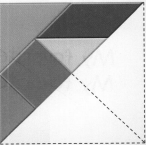

Page 125

Project Make a tangram.

a Use your tangram to make the pictures.

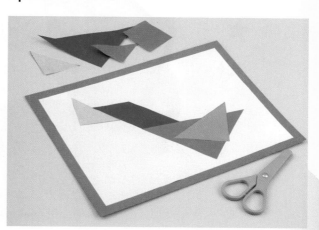

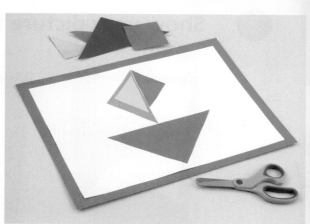

b Use your tangram to make a new picture.

1 **Listen and imagine. Then draw your picture.**

2 **Show your picture to your friends.**

This is my fantastic toy. It's a train. It's short. It's red and green.

The spelling game

1 CD 1 47 **Listen and look. Then listen and say the words.**

Pet show
bring your
pets!

1 elephant

2 rat

3 lizard

4 frog

5 spider

6 duck

7 dog

8 cat

2 CD 1 48 **Listen and chant.**

Pet show, pet show,
Look at all the pets.

Whisper and his spider,
Daisy and her dog,
Lenny and his lizard,
Sandra and her frog.

Donnie and his duck,
Katie and her cat,
Thunder and his elephant,
Misty and her rat.

Pet show, pet show,
Look at all the pets ...

1 CD1 49 Listen, read, and stick.

1

The green frog is on the desk.

2

The yellow frog is in the desk.

3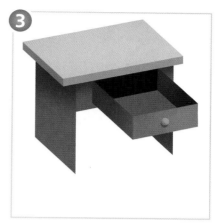

The red frog is under the desk.

2 CD1 50 Grammar focus Listen and say.

| The lizard is | in on under | the bag. |

3 Play the description game.

The spider …   Number …

1

2

3

4

5

6

7

8

9

10

Prepositions: *in, on, under*   **35**

1 CD 1 51 **Listen and sing.**

Look at the spiders,

Look at the rats,

Look at the lizards,

And look at the cats!

Look at the elephants,

Look at the dogs,

Look at the ducks,

And look at the frogs!

Spiders, cats,

Lizards, and rats.

Ducks, dogs,

Elephants, and frogs.

2 **Look at the picture. Count the animals. Where are they?**

Six spiders are on the pencil case.

1 CD 1 53 Listen and point to the pictures.

1
I like cats.
I don't like cats.

2
I don't like spiders.
I like spiders.

2 CD 1 54 Listen and circle what the spider says.

?

1

2

3

4

3 CD 1 55 Grammar focus — Listen and say.

☺ **I like** dogs.

☺ **I like** dogs, too.

☹ **I don't like** dogs.

4 Ask and answer.

I like … What about you?

I …

1

2

3

4

5

6

My brothers and sisters are on the tree!

Oh, no!

Aagh!

2 **Read and circle *yes* or *no*.**

1 In picture one Flash and Whisper like the spider.   yes / no

2 In picture three the spider is under the table.   yes / no

3 In picture four the spider is smart.   yes / no

4 In picture eight Misty, Thunder, and Flash like the spiders.   yes / no

3 **Find who says ...**  Touch him, Misty.

4 CD 1 59 **Listen and say.**

This is Tim and his silly sister Kim.

Skills

1 **Think!** **Read and circle the correct picture.**

Pet Show

Come and see the cats, dogs, rats, ducks, and lizards.

2 CD 1 61 Sticker **Listen and stick.**

3 **Write about the animals you like and don't like.**

I like rats and ducks. Ducks are my favorite!
I don't like dogs.

1 Listen to your teacher and stick.

Sticker

2 Look and say.

The cat is …

Speaking **41**

Camouflage

1 **What colors are the animals? Ask and answer.**

What color is the snake?

The snake is green and black.

snake   crocodile   butterfly   tiger   giraffe

2 **What animals are in the pictures?** There's a ... in picture one!

①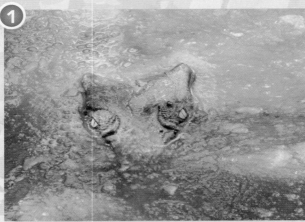

②

③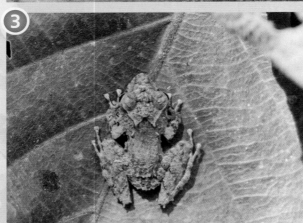

④

3 **Say why it is difficult to see the animals.**

The crocodile is green and the water is green.

1 **Think!** **Where do the animals hide?**

Tigers hide in tall grass.

1  **2**  **3**  **4**

logs

trees

leaves

tall grass

2 **Project** **Draw camouflage. Show it to your friends.**

Find and count the butterflies in my picture.

Do that!

1 CD1 63 **Listen and act it out with your teacher. Then listen again and number the pictures.**

2 **Read and number the sentences from the story.**

☐ Hug the little dog.   ☐ Listen.   ☐ Go to the door.

☐ He's cold. Pick him up.   ☐ There's a little dog under a tree.

☐ Open the door.

3 **Listen to your friend and act it out.**

There's a big spider under your book!

Quiz time

1 This is _____ .

   a a spider **b** a frog **c** a lizard

2 The cat is _____ the bag.

   a on **b** in **c** under

3 I _____ rats.

   a like **b** don't like

4 There are _____ ducks in the song.

   a seven **b** eight **c** nine

5 Whisper's pet is _____ .

   a a rat **b** a spider **c** a frog

6 Circle the word with the different sound.

   a Tim **b** him **c** spider

7 This is _____ .

   a a log **b** a leaf **c** grass

8 Tigers are _____ .

   a orange, white, and black

   b red, yellow, and brown

   c orange, black, and brown

1 CD 2 02 **Listen and look. Then listen and say the words.**

1 banana
2 cake
3 cheese sandwich
4 apple
5 pizza
6 sausage
7 chicken
8 steak
9 peas
10 carrots

2 CD 2 03 **Listen and chant.**

Lunchtime! Lunchtime!
What's for lunch?

I don't like chicken,
And I don't like cheese.
I don't like pizza,
And I don't like peas.

Lunchtime! Lunchtime!
What's for lunch?

Oh, I like apples,
And I like steak.
Oh, I like carrots,
And I like cake!
Yummy!

1 Read and draw lines.

1 I have a sandwich and an apple.

2 I have a sandwich and a banana.

3 I have pizza and a banana. I don't have an apple.

4 I have pizza and an apple. I don't have a banana.

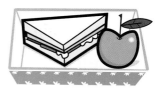
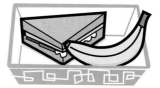

2 CD2 04 Grammar focus Listen and say.

I **have** a sandwich and **an** apple.
I **don't have** a banana.

3 Choose your lunch. Find a friend with the same lunch.

 Sticker

I have …   Me, too!

1 CD2 06 **Listen and sing.**

Tommy's in the kitchen,
Come and take him out!
Tommy's in the kitchen,
Come and take him out!

I have an apple in my sandwich.
I have milk on my peas.
I have juice on my sausage.
Help! Oh, help me, please!

Tommy's in the kitchen ...

I have carrots on my pizza.
And a banana on my cheese.
I have chicken with my cake.
Help! Oh, help me, please!

Tommy's in the kitchen ...

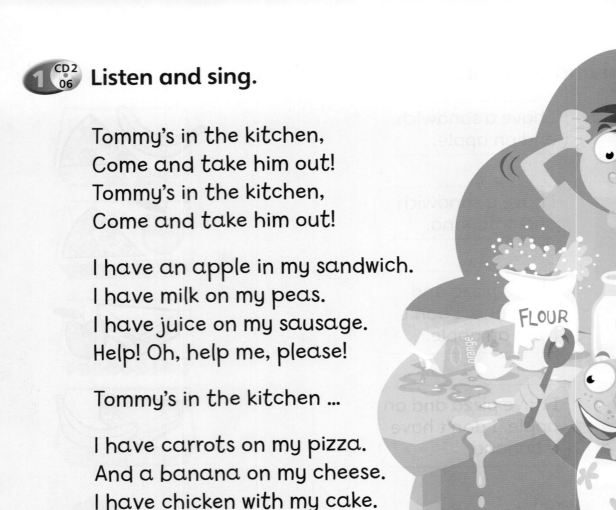

2 CD2 08 **Listen again and draw lines to match Tommy's food.**

1 CD2 09 **Listen and check (✓) or put an X in the box.**

1

2

2 CD2 10 Grammar focus **Listen and say.**

Do we have **any** cheese?   Yes, we **do**.
No, we **don't**.

3 **Ask and answer.**

Do we have any ... ?

2 Read and check (✓) or put an X.

Who says … ?				
I have pizza.				
I have an apple.				
I have a sausage.				
I have peas.				
I have a banana.				

3 Find who says … Nice and hot.

4 Listen and say.

Polly stops to get a hot dog from Todd.

1 CD 2 15 **Listen and say the numbers.**

eleven   twelve   thirteen   fourteen   fifteen

sixteen   seventeen   eighteen   nineteen   twenty

2 CD 2 16 **Listen and complete the shopping list.**

Shopping list

12 apples

3 **Write a shopping list.**

Shopping list

13 *steaks*

4 **Listen to your partner's list and write it down.
Check your list.**

1 **Look and read. Write *yes* or *no*.**

1 Mark: I have eleven sausages in my basket. _____

2 Tony: I have fourteen apples in my basket. _____

3 Lynn: I don't have any bananas in my basket. _____

4 Mark: I have chicken in my basket. _____

5 Tony: I have a cheese sandwich in my basket. _____

6 Lynn: I have twelve carrots in my basket. _____

2 **Draw your basket. Say what's in it.**

I have ten cupcakes in my basket!

Fruit and Veg

1 Look at the fruit and vegetables. Which are your favorites?

It is important to eat fruit and vegetables to be healthy.

> Pears are my favorite fruit.

> Corn is my favorite vegetable.

broccoli

onions

peaches

pineapples

mushrooms

pears

oranges

green beans

potatoes

coconuts

tomatoes

corn

vegetables

fruit

2   **Think!** Look and stick. Are they fruit or vegetables?

Learn and think

1 **Think!** **Where do they grow? Follow the lines and say.**

Onions grow in the ground.   Coconuts grow on trees.

1  **2**  **3**  **4**  **5**

a  **b**  **c**  **d**  **e**

tree   tree   plant   ground   plant

2 **Project** **Make a fruit and vegetable diary.**

How many fruits and vegetables do you eat every day?

	Day 1	Day 2	Day 3	Day 4	Day 5	Day 6	Day 7
fruits							
vegetables							

Create that!

1 **Listen and imagine. Then draw your picture.**

2 **Write about your picture. Then listen to your friends and guess.**

Hi, I'm Pop. I'm a monster. Here's my sandwich.
I have a plane, a train, and a go-cart in it. Yummy!

The lunchbox game

I have a ...

fruit

vegetable

sandwich

drink

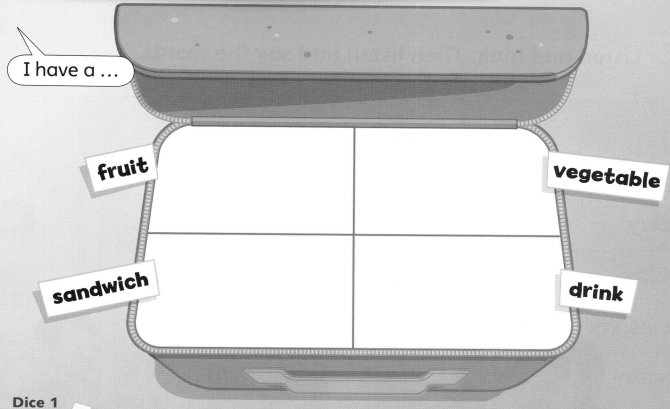

5 Free time

1 CD2 18 **Listen and look. Then listen and say the words.**

This week

1	Monday	School
2	Tuesday	School
3	Wednesday	School
4	Thursday	School
5	Friday	School

6	Saturday	Soccer game
7	Sunday	Trip to the lake

2 CD2 19 **Listen and chant.**

Hooray, hooray!
School on Monday,
School on Tuesday,
School on Wednesday,
Thursday, Friday.

On Saturday and Sunday,
More time to play.

School is cool.
Hooray, hooray!

1 CD 2 20 Listen and stick.

Sandra	Pat	Maria	Oliver	Bill

2 CD 2 21 Grammar focus Listen and say.

I **go swimming** on Mondays.
I **play soccer** on Saturdays.

3 Ask and answer.

I … on Mondays. What about you?

I … on Mondays.

1 CD2 23 **Listen and sing.**

It's a busy, busy, busy, busy,
Busy, busy, busy week ...

On Mondays we go swimming.
On Tuesdays we play ball.
On Wednesdays and on Thursdays,
We play computer games.

On Fridays we play soccer.
On Saturdays we sing.
On Sundays we play hide-and-seek.
Oh, what a busy week!

It's a busy, busy, busy, busy,
Busy, busy, busy week ...

Oh yeah!

2 **Point to the pictures and say the day of the week.**

It's Friday.

1 **Listen and circle the answer.**

Do you watch TV
on the weekend?

Yes, I do. No, I don't.

Do you play
computer games
on the weekend?

Yes, I do. No, I don't.

2 **Grammar focus** **Listen and say.**

Do you watch TV on the weekend? **Yes, I do.**
No, I don't.

3 **Play the question game.**

Do you … on the weekend? Yes, I do.

Value: asking for help when you need it

7 Are you OK, rabbit?

8 Now, I'm lost.

Now, he's lost!

2 Think! **Look at the picture and choose the correct sentence.**

?

1 Are you OK?

2 Come with me.

3 Here you go.

4 I'm lost.

3 **Find who says …** This isn't much fun.

4 CD 2 29 **Listen and say.**

Justine jumps in the mud with the ducks.

Skills

1 CD2 31 **Look at the picture. Listen and write a name or a number.**

1 What is the name of Mark's school? _____

2 What is the name of Mark's brother? _____

3 What is the name of Mark's teacher? _____

4 How many days do Mark and his friends play soccer? _____

5 How many days do Mark and his friends go swimming? _____

6 How many days do Mark and his friends play computer games? _____

Skills

1 **Read and say the poem.**

My perfect week

On Mondays
I play with friends.

On Tuesdays
I ride my bike.

On Wednesdays
I play computer games.

On Thursdays
I play with toys.

On Fridays
I go swimming.

On Saturdays and Sundays
I watch TV and sleep.

That's my perfect week.

2 **Write your poem.**

My perfect week
On Mondays
I watch TV ...

I'm healthy!

1 CD 2 33 **Listen and read. Ask and answer.**

MILK

For a healthy life, it is important to:

- Have fun
- Eat healthy food
- Stay in shape
- Play sports
- Learn new things
- Sleep

Sketch

1 How do you have fun?

I play with my friends.

2 How do you stay in shape?

3 How do you learn new things?

2 **Look at the pictures and draw lines.**

1

2

3

healthy   unhealthy

4

5

6

1 Project **Do the class survey.**

a Ask and answer. Check (✓) the boxes.

How many hours a week do you play sports?

I play sports four hours a week.

How many hours a week do you ...	1–2 hours	3–4 hours	5–6 hours	7+ hours
play sports?				
watch TV?				
play with friends?				
read books?				
play computer games?				

b Make a bar chart and show it to your friends.

Four people play sports three or four hours a week.

PLAY SPORTS

WATCH TV

Do that!

1 CD2 34 **Listen and act it out with your teacher. Then listen again and number the pictures.**

☐  ☐  ☐

☐  ☐  ☐

2 **Read and number the sentences from the story.**

☐ Oh, no! Cover your ears. ☐ Start playing the piano.

☐ Sit down at the piano. ☐ Put it on the floor.

☐ Open the piano. ☐ Look! Your cat is in the piano.

3 **Listen to your friend and act it out.**

Start riding your bike.

1 Make a poster.

Our week

a Write the days of the week on your poster.

b Think of things you do during the week and find pictures.

c Cut out the pictures and stick them on your poster.

2 Look at the posters. Ask and answer.

I play soccer. What day of the week is it?

It's Tuesday.

6 The old house

1 CD2 35 **Listen and look. Then listen and say the words.**

1 bathroom   2 bedroom

3 living room   4 hallway   5 dining room   6 kitchen

7 stairs   8 cellar

2 CD2 36 **Listen and chant.**

Let's go to the old house,
The old house, the old house.
Let's go to the old house,
Let's go now!

What's in the bedroom?
What's in the bathroom?
What's in the kitchen?
Let's find out!

What's in the living room?
What's in the dining room?
What's in the cellar?
Let's find out!

Down the stairs,
Open the door,
Aagh!

6

1 **Listen and match the monsters with their bedrooms.**

2   **Listen and say.**

> **There's** a monster.   **There are** four cats.

3 **Think!** **Play the description game.**

(There's a monster and there …)   (Number …)

1  **Listen and sing.**

Come on, come on and see me,
In my little house.
There are lots of nice animals,
In my little house.

There's a cat in the living room.
There's a spider in the kitchen.
There are seven crocodiles,
In my nice bathroom.

Come on, come on and see me ...

There's a snake in the cellar.
There's a lizard in my bedroom.
There are tigers, lots of tigers,
In my nice yard.

Come on, come on and see me ...

2 **Listen again and number the pictures.**

1 Listen, look, and stick.

Sticker

1 Is there a park?	
2 Are there any bikes?	
3 Are there any dogs?	
4 How many ducks are there?	

2 CD2 44 Grammar focus Listen and say.

Is there a plane?	Yes, there is.
Are there any rats?	No, there aren't.
How many cars are there?	There are four cars.

3 Look at Activity 1 again. Ask and answer.

Is there a ... ?

Yes, there is.

1  2  3  4

5  6  7   8

7 There's no problem, you can come in.

Misty, where are you?

8 Here I am.

Aagh!

Help!

2 **Make sentences with a friend.**

In picture one there's a house.

In picture three there are eight stairs.

3 **Find who says ...** Help!

4 CD 2 47 **Listen and say.**

Harry's **h**allway is full of **h**ats.

1 **Look, read, and write *a*, *b*, *c*, or *d*.**

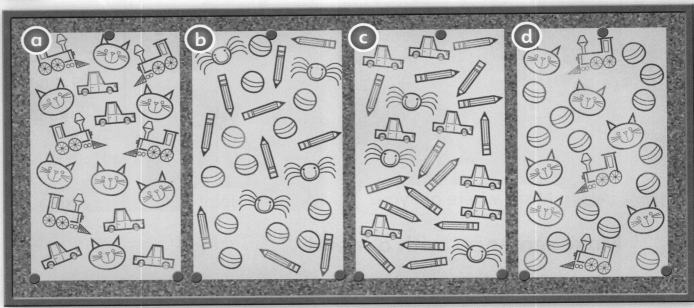

1 There are 15 pencils. ____

2 There are five trains. ____

3 There are seven cars. ____

4 There are four spiders. ____

5 There are 14 balls. ____

6 There are six cats. ____

2 **Look at the pictures again. Ask and answer.**

How many cats are there in picture a?

There are seven.

Skills

1 CD 2 50 **Listen and check (✓) the correct picture.**

1

 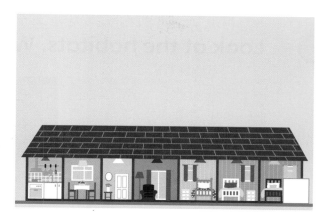

2

3

 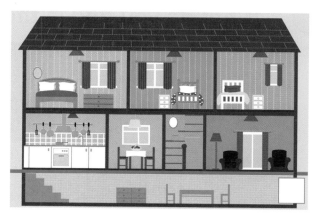

2 **Write about your house.**

I live in a nice house. There are three bedrooms, a kitchen, a dining room, a living room, and a hallway. There isn't a cellar. I like my house.

 # HABITATS

1 Look at the habitats. What colors are they?

polar region

ocean

The polar region is white and blue.

jungle

desert

mountains

2 What do you find in the habitats?

sand

trees

You find sand in the desert.

rocks

coral

snow

78 Geography

1 **Think!** **Where do you find the animals?**

You find tigers in the jungle.

tiger

parrot

camel

goat

polar bear

shark

jellyfish

penguin

2 **Project** **Make a habitat.**

1 CD2 51 **Listen and imagine. Then draw your picture.**

2 **Show your picture to your friends.**

This is my house. There are five bedrooms.

Yes, there is.

Is there a yard?

Quiz time

1 What is this?

   a a hallway   b a dining room   c a cellar

2 There _____ three bedrooms.

   a is   b are

3 Where is the lizard in the song?

   a in the bathroom   b in the bedroom

   c in the kitchen

4 How many cats are there in the bag?

   a 2   b 3   c 4

5 Who isn't scared of the house?

a    b    c

6 How many rats are there in the house?

   a 7   b 8   c 9

7 Which word has a different sound?

   a **h**at   b **h**elp   c **sh**oe

8 Where do you find coral?

   a in the ocean   b in the mountains

   c in the jungle

7 Get dressed!

Listen and look. Then listen and say the words.

1 jeans
2 sweater
3 jacket
4 skirt
5 shorts
6 cap
7 shoes
8 socks
9 T-shirt
10 pants

2 CD 3 03 **Listen and chant.**

Put on your T-shirt.
Put on your pants.
Put on your sweater.
Put on your socks.
Put on your shoes.
Put on your cap,
And now let's rap!

T-shirt, pants,
Sweater, shoes,
Socks and cap.
Do the clothes rap!

Come on, Whisper,
Time for school!

1 CD3 04 **Look at the pictures and draw lines. Then listen and check.**

1 Do you like these shoes?

2 No, I don't.

3 Yes, I do.

4 Do you like this T-shirt?

2 CD3 05 **Grammar focus** **Listen and say.**

Do you like this hat?   **Yes, I do.**
Do you like these shoes?   **No, I don't.**

3 **Look at the clothes. Ask and answer.**

Do you like … ?   Yes, I do.

1
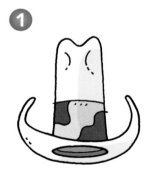

2

3

4

5

6

7

8

1 CD3 06 **Listen and sing.**

I'm a cool, cool cat.
Meow, meow, meow!
I like this super hat.
I'm a cool, cool cat.

Cool shoes and cool jackets,
Cool socks and super shorts,
Cool T-shirts and cool sweaters,
And cool, cool skirts.

We're cool, cool cats.
Meow, meow, meow!
We like these super hats.
We're cool, cool cats ...
Meow!

2 **Look at the picture and say the color of the clothes.**

This hat is pink.

These socks are red.

1 CD3 08 **Listen and write the names.** Lara Emma Paul Ken

2 CD3 09 **Grammar focus** **Listen and say.**

Olivia's wear**ing** a red sweater.
Is he wear**ing** a blue T-shirt? Yes, he **is**.
Is she wear**ing** brown shoes? No, she **isn't**.

3 **Play the guessing game.**

It's a boy.

Hmm. Is he wearing a blue T-shirt?

2 Think! **Look at the picture and choose the correct sentence.**

1 Oh, no!

2 My coat isn't here.

3 Can you get my ball?

4 She's wearing my T-shirt!

3 **Find who says …** Stop!

4 CD 3 12 **Listen and say.**

Six **sp**iders **st**op for sandwiches on the **st**airs.

1 **Look and read. Write *yes* or *no*.**

1 Naomi is wearing a black skirt. _____

2 James is wearing a red hat. _____

3 David is wearing a blue and red sweater. _____

4 Oscar is wearing a blue cap. _____

5 Amy is wearing a blue skirt and red socks. _____

6 Hannah is wearing green socks and black sneakers. _____

Skills

1 **Think!** **Ask and answer.**

Is Tom riding a pony?

No, I think he's riding a bike.

| Tom: ride | Emma: play | Kylie: eat | Fred: play |

2 CD3 14 **Listen, check, and stick.**

3 **Look at Activity 1 again. Choose and write.**

Tom is wearing a blue helmet, a green jacket, black pants, and red shoes. He is riding a bike.

4 **Play the mime game. Are you Tom, Emma, Kylie, or Fred?**

Who am I?

You're ...

Learn and think

Materials

1 CD 3 15 **Listen, read, and draw lines.**

Cotton comes from plants. You can wear cotton shorts and T-shirts.
Leather comes from cows. You can wear leather shoes and jackets.
Wool comes from sheep. You can wear wool sweaters and socks.

1

4

2

5

3

6

2 **Think!** **Say the material for the clothes.** Picture one is wool.

1  **2**  **3**  **4** **5**  **6**

1 Look, read, and write the words.

| cool | strong | warm |

1 Wool is _____ .

2 Leather is _____ .

3 Cotton is _____ .

2  Make a poster with different materials.

Science **91**

1 CD3 16 **Listen and act it out with your teacher. Then listen again and number the pictures.**

2 **Read and number the sentences from the story.**

☐ Turn around.

☐ Put the fly outside.

☐ Catch the fly.

☐ Oh, no! The fly is on your nose.

☐ Open the window.

☐ You can see a fly on your jeans.

3 **Listen to your friend and act it out.**

Put the bird outside.

The dressing game

8 The robot

1 CD 3 17 **Listen and look. Then listen and say the words.**

1 head

2 arm

3 fingers

4 hand

5 knee

6 leg

7 toes

8 foot

2 CD 3 18 **Listen and chant.**

Let's make a robot!
Here's the head.
Here's an arm.
Here's a hand.
Here are the fingers.

Here's a leg.
Here's a knee.
Here's a foot.
Here are the toes.
Thank you! Off it goes.

1 CD3 19 **Look and listen. What can Misty do?**

I can't touch my toes.

I can't jump rope.

I can't stand on one leg.

2 Sticker **Read and stick. Help the Super Friends see Misty.**

I can touch my toes.

I can jump rope.

I can stand on one leg.

3 CD3 20 **Grammar focus** **Listen and say.**

I **can** stand on one leg.
She **can** jump rope.

I **can't** touch my toes.
He **can't** jump rope.

4 **Make sentences.**

Anna can …

I can …

Anna

Pete

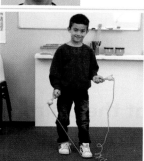

1 CD 3 / 21 **Listen and sing.**

Larry Lizard

Bella Bird

Can you guess who we are?
Can you guess who we are?
Listen and say who we are!

Who am I?
I can sing.
Who am I?
I can swim.
Who am I?
I can jump up high.

Who am I?
I can run.
Who am I?
I can dance.
Who am I?
I can crawl and fly.

Can you guess who we are? ...

Dan Dolphin

Kate Kangaroo

Lucy Ladybug

Charlie Cheetah

2 CD 3 / 23 **Listen again and say what the animals can do.**

It's Bella Bird. She can sing.

CD 3 24 **Look and say. Then listen and check (✓) or put an X.**

play the piano   swim   ride a horse
ride a bike   play tennis   dance

> Number one is *play tennis*.

	①	②	③	④	⑤	⑥
Sophie						
Tom						

 CD 3 25 **Grammar focus** **Listen and say.**

Can you swim?   Yes, I **can**.
Can you dance?   No, I **can't**.

3 **Play the action game.**

Can you … ?

Can you … ?

1

Give me the right leg and the left arm.

Here's the right leg.

Here's the left arm.

2

And now the head, please.

Here's the head.

3

Batteries! We don't have batteries.

No problem.

4

Here you go.

Thank you.

5

Robot, can you speak?

Nac I sey.

6

We have a problem.

It can't speak.

Let me try something.

2 **Think!** **What does the robot say?**

koob   smra

toof

ekib

miws

3 **Find who says ...** Give me the right leg.

4 CD 3 28 **Listen and say.**

Greg has a bi**g** ba**g** and a **g**reen **g**o-cart.

 Phonics focus **99**

Skills

1 **Listen and check (✓) the box.**

1 Can Patch swim?

a  **b**

2 Can Sue ride a bike?

a  **b**

3 Can Coco stand on one leg?

a  **b**

2 **Ask your friends what they can do.**

Can you … ?	Name
play the piano	
speak Spanish	
ride a horse	
play the guitar	

Skills

1 **Look, read, and draw lines.**

a I'm an Octo. I have one head. I have two legs and eight arms. I can dance.

b I'm a Klump. I have two heads. I have six legs and I can run very fast, but I can't jump.

c I'm a Dook. I have two heads. I have five legs and I have ten feet. I can jump!

d I'm a Zak. I have one head, eight legs, and four wings. I can fly, but I can't jump.

1

2

3

4

2 **Draw a funny animal and write about it.**

I'm a Brog.
I have three heads,
three legs, and four
arms. I'm green.
I can dance.

The Skeleton

1 CD 3 32 **Listen and read. Write the words.**

On this page you can see skeletons. Humans and some animals have skeletons. The skeleton helps us swim, walk, run, sit, and stand.

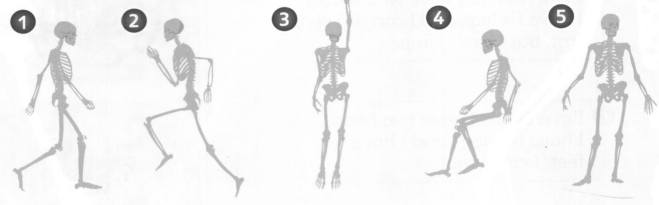

2 **Look and match the animals with their skeletons.**

⑧

1 What do you think? Read and answer.

The skeleton has lots of bones. They are strong. Can you feel them?

1 How many bones are in your arm?
  a 1   **b** 2   **c** 3

2 How many bones are in your finger?
  a 1   **b** 2   **c** 3

2 Think! Look at the bones and find them in your body.

1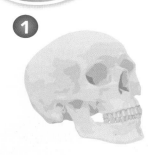

2

3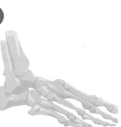

4

head   knee   foot   arm

3 Project Put the cutouts together to make a skeleton.

Page 127

This is the head.

Create that!

1 CD3 33 **Listen and imagine. Then draw your picture.**

2 **Write about your picture. Then listen to your friends and guess.**

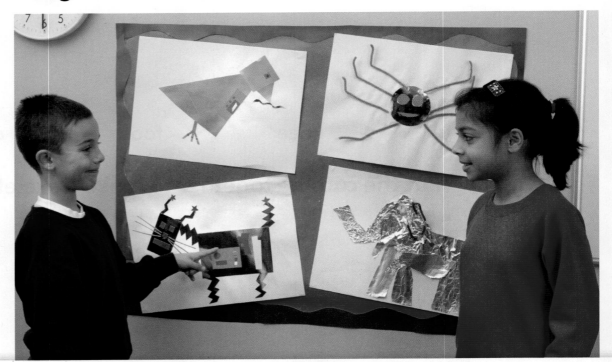

My robot pet is a cat. It has a nice head. It has four legs and a long tail. It has big ears. It can dance. Its name is Robocat.

1 **Make a poster.**

Our body

a Write *Our body* on your poster.

b Think of parts of the body and find pictures.

c Cut out the pictures and stick them on your poster.

2 **Play the memory game.**

> There is a boy and a girl. The boy has …

⑨ At the beach

1 [CD3 34] **Listen and look. Then listen and say the words.**

1) catch a fish

2) paint a picture

3) eat ice cream

4) take a picture

5) listen to music

6) look for shells

7) read a book

8) make a sandcastle

2 [CD3 35] **Listen and chant.**

Eat ice cream,
Yum, yum.
Take pictures,
Click, click.
Catch fish,
Splish, splash.

Make castles,
Dig, dig.
Look for shells,
Look, look.
Play in the sun,
It's lots of fun!

1 CD 3 36 Listen and number the pictures. Then write the words.

paint   take   look   listen

☐ Let's _____ to music.

Good idea.

☐ Let's _____ a picture.

I'm not sure.

☐ Let's _____ for shells.

Sorry, I don't want to.

☐ Let's _____ a picture.

Good idea.

2 CD 3 37 Grammar focus   Listen and say.

Let's **play** the guitar.

Good idea.
I'm not sure.
Sorry, I don't want to.

3 Look and act it out.

Let's ...

Good idea.

1
2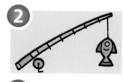
3
4
5
6

1 CD3 38 **Listen and sing.**

Let's go to the beach.
Let's look for shells.
Let's play in the sand.
Let's run hand in hand ...

It's vacation time,
It's vacation time,
For you and me.

Let's take a picture.
Let's catch a fish.
Let's swim in the sun,

Fun, fun, fun! ...

It's vacation time ...

2 CD3 40 **Listen again and number the pictures.**

1 ^{CD 3 41} Listen and read. Check (✓) the correct picture.

a

1 Where's the shell?

It's on the sandcastle.

b

a

2 Where are the kites?

They're in the blue and yellow toy box.

b

2 ^{CD 3 42} **Grammar focus** Listen and say.

Where's the blue book? **It's** in the green bag.
Where **are** the orange books? **They're** in the black bag.

3 Play the question game.

Where's … ?   It's …

1

2

3

4

5

6

1

2

3

4

5

6

7 "Now you can race to the top, Flash!"

"No. Let's go together. That's more fun!"

8 "What a good idea!"

"Yes!"

2 (Think!) **Read and write the names.**

1 I'm super! _____

2 A race? I'm not happy about that. _____

3 Flash can't see it! _____

4 I really like my friends. _____

3 **Find who says ...** "Just wait and see."

4 CD 3 45 **Listen and say.**

Jean keeps her teeth really clean.

1 **Read and write the country.**

Come to Australia. Make a sandcastle on the beautiful beaches. See the animals: the kangaroo and the koala. Swim and snorkel in the ocean.

Come to Canada. Catch a fish in one of the beautiful lakes. Take a picture of the big forests and high mountains. Watch the whales or go horseback riding.

Come to the U.K. See Buckingham Palace and the famous Tower Bridge in England. Go to Scotland and listen to the music of bagpipes.

a _____ b _____ c _____

2 CD3 47 **Listen and check (✓) the country.**

	1	2	3	4	5	6

3 **Write about your country.**

Come to Mexico. See the beautiful beaches and swim in the ocean.

Skills

1 Sticker

Listen to your teacher and stick.

2 **Look and say.** The ice cream is …

Vacation Weather

1 **Look and talk about the weather.**

It's sunny and hot.

 a
 b
 c
 d
 e
 f

2 Think! **Read the sentences and write the countries on the map.**

1 It's hot and sunny in Mexico.

2 It's cold and snowing in Scotland.

3 It's raining in Japan.

4 It's cloudy in Italy.

Learn and think

1 Read and draw lines. Write the countries on the postcards.

1
Dear Nathan,
My vacation is great. It's snowing.
It's very cold, but it's fun.
Daisy

a

_____

2
Dear Emily,
It's hot here. Very hot. It's sunny.
I love it! How are you?
Dylan

b

_____

3
Dear Adam,
It's raining here, but it's very beautiful. See
you soon.
Your friend, Andrea

c

_____

2 Project Write a weather diary.

Do that!

1 CD 3 49 **Listen and act it out with your teacher. Then listen again and number the pictures.**

☐  ☐  ☐

☐  ☐  ☐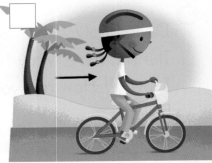

2 **Read and number the sentences from the story.**

☐ Goodbye, ice cream! ☐ Ride to the beach.

☐ You trip over your helmet. ☐ Get an ice-cream cone.

☐ Stop and put your helmet on the ground. ☐ You're hot.

3 **Listen to your friend and act it out.**

Make a sandcastle.

Quiz time

1 Let's _____ a sandcastle.
  a eat   b take   c make

2 Let's _____ .
  a play the guitar   b swim in the ocean
  c paint a picture

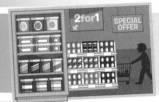

3 Where _____ the ice cream?
  a is   b are

4 Who wants to race?

a    b    c

5 Who wins the race?
  a Thunder   b Flash   c all the Super Friends

6 Which word has a different sound?
  a ch**ee**se   b p**e**t   c b**ea**ch

7 Where do you find koalas?
  a in the U.K.   b in Australia   c in Canada

8 What's the weather like?
  a It's hot.   b It's cloudy.   c It's sunny.

Holidays and cutouts

HALLOWEEN

Christmas

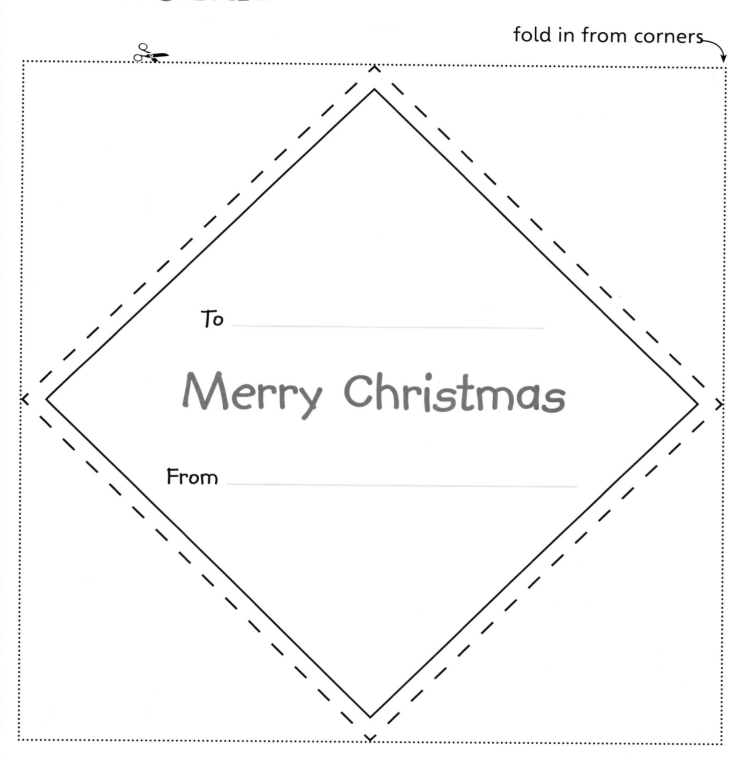

fold in from corners

To _____

Merry Christmas

From _____

fold in from corners

Easter

Unit 2 Cutout (page 31)

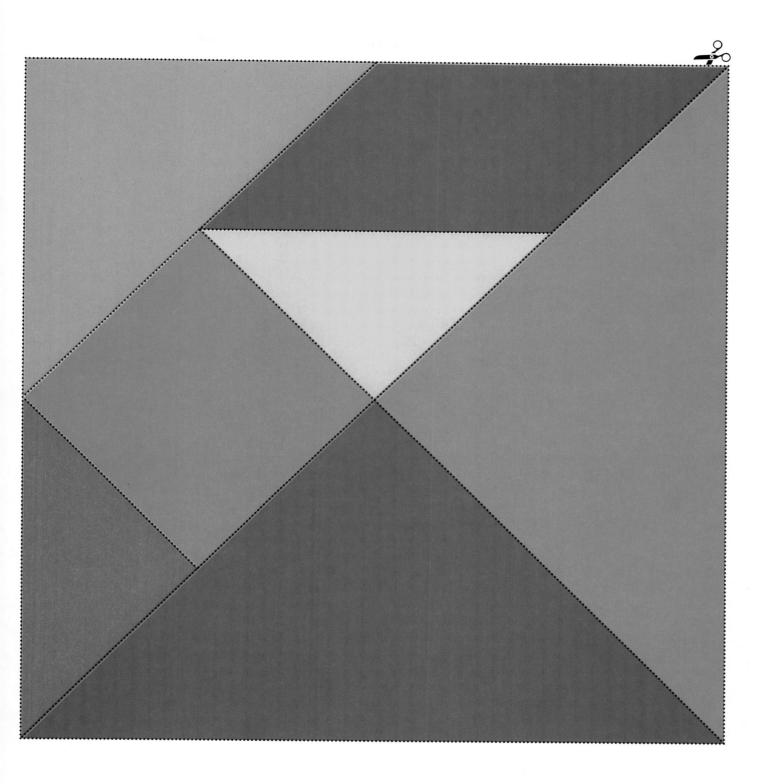

Unit 8 Cutout (page 103)

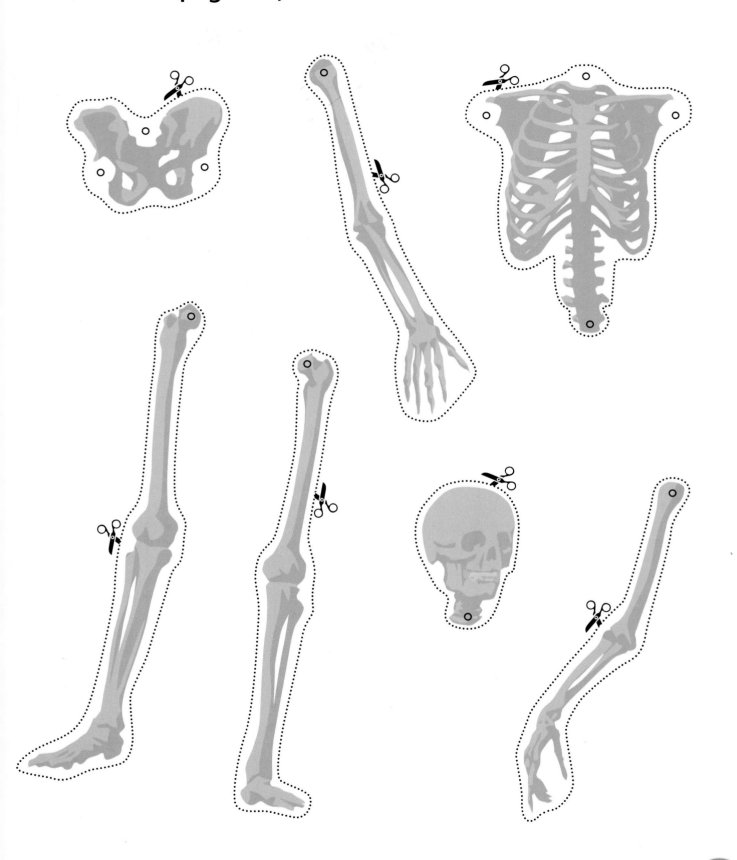